MiG-29
SOVIET SUPERFIGHTER

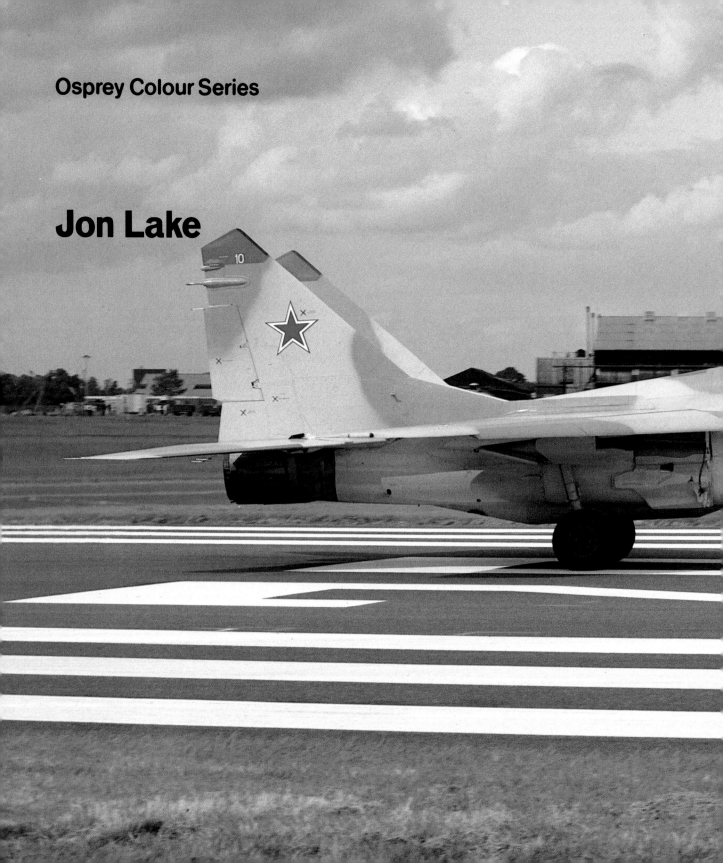

Osprey Colour Series

Jon Lake

MiG-29
SOVIET SUPERFIGHTER

Published in 1989 by Osprey Publishing
Limited
59 Grosvenor Street, London W1X 9DA

British Library Cataloguing in Publication
Data

Lake, Jon
    MiG-29: Soviet Superfighter
    1. Aeroplanes, 29 MiG
    I. Title
    623.74'63
ISBN 0-85045-920-6

Editor Dennis Baldry
Designed by Martin Richards
Printed in Hong Kong

Front cover Mikoyan test pilot
Roman Taskaev probably flew the
finest knife-edge pass ever seen at
Farnborough, a manoeuvre which
again demonstrated the aircraft's
generous thrust-to-weight ratio as
well as the amount of lift generated
by the fuselage, engine intake trunks
and tail fins

Back cover After an impressively
short take-off run (reportedly 240 m),
Mikoyan test pilot Roman Taskaev
heaves back on the pole as his MiG-
29 blasts into the air during
Farnborough week in 1988

Title pages The MiG-29 waits on
the 'piano keys' of Farnborough's
main runway before take-off. The
most obvious features of the aircraft
are its deeply humped cockpit and
forward fuselage, short main
undercarriage with legs set well
forward, and the huge blanked-off
engine intakes (the latter feature not
visible in this almost perfect side
view). Close up, the aircraft often
described as an F/A-18 Hornet copy
could be seen to be a bird of a very
different feather

Right Mean, moody and
magnificent. This head-on view of
the MiG-29 emphasizes its sleek but
deadly lines

Contents

Acknowledgements

Jon Lake is employed as an Editor by a British aviation publisher, and has contributed articles and photographs to many magazines. Aviation and photography have been lifelong interests, and he has a particular interest in Soviet aeroplanes. An enthusiastic RAF-trained private pilot he has flown in and photographed several fast jet types and hopes one day to fly in the MiG-29. 'Photography would take a back seat to trying my hand at that tailslide!' he confided, and I don't know whether he was joking!

This book would have been impossible without the generous assistance, advice and encouragement of a host of friends. Special thanks go to Jilly Foreman, Bill Gunston, Squadron Leader Tony Paxton, Hasse Vallas, Bob Dorr, Denis J Calvert, Pushpindar Singh, Emil Pozar, Bill Green, Gordon Swanborough, Mike Badrocke, Paul Blanchard, Allan Burney, Big Bill Beadsmoore, Patrick Bunce, Grant Race, Ian Rentoul, Robert Ruffle, Tom Wakeford, Dick Ward and Chris Allan and to Air Commodore Dan Honley and Mr Duncan Simpson of the SBAC. Thanks are also due to my colleagues Dave, Rod, Johnny, Lee and Paul who endured hours of *Fulcrum* conversation. I hope it didn't spoil too many pints, chaps! Above all, thanks to Rostislav Belyakov, Mikhail Waldenburg, Roman Taskaev, Anatoly Kvotchur and Alexander Velovich of the Mikoyan OKB, whose patience and kindness were an unexpected bonus at Farnborough 1988. For those interested my photos were taken on a Canon T-90 using Kodachrome 64 and Kodachrome 200 film, the others on a variety of equipment.

Glasnost greetings: the MiG-29UB combat trainer leads the single seater through cloudly English skies en route to Farnborough on 30 August 1988 (*Tony Paxton*)

Introduction

There has long been a widespread and erroneous belief that the Mikoyan MiG-29 is inferior to contemporary Western fighters. It has been grudgingly admitted that the MiG-29 is a much better aircraft than the aircraft it is replacing, and that the West's qualitative lead has probably been eroded. However, most people have assumed that the new aircraft is little more than a clever extrapolation of Western designs, a Soviet F/A-18 Hornet incorporating some F-14 and F-15 aerodynamics, and equipped with a weapons system which is a slavish copy of the APG-65. The visit by six MiG-29s to Finland, and reports from India prompted a slight reappraisal, and people began to realise that the MiG-29 is a much more formidable aircraft than previously supposed.

The MiG-29's dramatic appearance at Farnborough added more evidence of this remarkable aircraft's capabilities, and it is now possible to evaluate realistically the *Fulcrum*. At least as manoeuvrable as the F-16, with better high alpha performance, the MiG-29 is also capable of operating from much shorter, more primitive airstrips. Its sophisticated intakes allow it to exceed Mach 2, and it has a faster rate of climb. Its AA-10 *Alamo* missiles give the MiG-29 a superior BVR (beyond visual range) capability. A helmet-mounted sighting system allows true off-boresight missile firing capability, freeing the *Fulcrum* pilot from pointing his nose at the target to 'lock it up'. Finally the integrated fire control system allows the MiG-29 pilot to detect and track, then lock on to and launch his missiles against a target without using his radar.

In short, the MiG-29 is the best all-round air superiority fighter in the world . . . probably.

Fulcrum
in Finland

Before 1 July 1986, most people in
the West had only seen a single
grainy satellite image of the MiG-29,
although the aircraft had made its
maiden flight during 1977, and had
entered service in 1983. The new
fighter was eventually revealed to the
West during a squadron exchange
visit with HavLv 31, Finland's MiG-21
equipped fighter unit. Here the six
MiG-29s are seen on arrival at
Kuopio Rissala, escorted by a single
Finnish MiG-21*bis*

Squadron exchanges between Kubinka-based MiG units and HavLv 31 have occurred every four years since the first visit by the Finns in 1973. The first reciprocal visit by a Soviet regiment took place in 1974. When they arrived at Kuopio Rissala the detachment commander, Colonel Longinenko, led the Kubinka-based MiG-29s in a formation flypast before they landed

The MiG-29s which visited Finland were flown by six very senior and experienced pilots, none of them below the rank of Major. This gave rise to much speculation that they were from a specialized trials and demonstration unit

The aircraft which visited Finland were fitted with the original narrow chord rudders, and had an ILS antenna mounted on the fairing under the nose. Interestingly the aircraft were not fitted with nosewheel mudguards, unlike virtually all other Soviet tactical fighters

From the rear the MiG-29 does bear a passing resemblance to the McDonnell Douglas F-15 Eagle, although the widely spaced engine nacelles are more similar to those of the Grumman F-14 Tomcat. The MiG-29, is however a superb original design in its own right, and not just a copy or 'composite' of any Western fighters

09.58, Kuopio Rissala air base, Finland. Some of the local bird life takes flight as the first pair of red-starred 'Eagles' howl down the approach. A long, flat and rather fast approach is flown by the MiG-29, as seen here on approach to Kuopio Rissala

Left Major Kravets taxies in, displaying the distinctive lines of his MiG-29, '07'. Western observers were fascinated by the Infra Red Search and Track System carried by the MiG-29, served by a glass ball mounted on top of the nose. Inevitable speculative comparisons with the system carried by the F-102 Delta Dagger followed!

Below Four of the MiG-29s gave a polished display of formation flying at Kuopio Rissala, starting with an impressively short formation take-off. The formation was led by the deputy detachment commander, Lieutenant Colonel V Iachin, with Majors Solovyev and Kravets as Nos 2 and 3 and with Major Arastov in the box

Right Major Vladimir Chilin lands after his breathtaking solo aerobatic display at Kuopio Rissala. A huge cruciform braking parachute helped bring the fighter to a halt. The massive underslung air intakes were closed off by huge doors, which seemed to be triggered by weight on the nosewheels

Below right The MiG-29 visit to Finland was considered a remarkable departure from traditional Soviet secrecy, but although they allowed their aircraft to be photographed, only Finnish Air Force personnel were able to inspect the aircraft at close quarters, and no performance figures, technical details, or even dimensions were released to the press

As Major Chilin finished his landing roll the formation of four MiG-29s thundered in to give their display. With the MiG-29, as with other tactical aircraft intended for operation from semi-prepared frontline airfields, the Mikoyan Design Bureau preferred to fit a braking parachute rather than opt for the heavier and more complex option of using thrust reversers, as fitted to the Swedish Saab Viggen and trinational Panavia Tornado. The *Ilmavoimat* (Finnish Air Force) has a long-standing requirement for a fighter to replace its MiG-21s and Drakens, and the Soviet Union used the long established squadron exchange as an opportunity to mount an impromptu sales demonstration

Left Many were surprised by the unusual camouflage scheme applied to the MiG-29, which seemed to change colour slightly under different lighting conditions, sometimes appearing to have a distinctive green bias, and at other times appearing to be a bluish grey. Some of the Soviet pilots had large red stars emblazoned on their flying helmets, a far cry from the gaudy bone domes worn by some USN pilots, perhaps, but nevertheless an unusual departure for Frontal Aviation, where personal and even unit markings have previously always been discouraged

Right In Finland the Soviet pilots tended to deploy their braking parachutes as the aircraft touched down, which is the normal operating technique where landing distances are not critical. The 'chute is stored in a small cylinder in the flat 'beaver tail' between the jetpipes, and deploys with a sharp 'crack' (All photos in 'Fulcrum in Finland' by Hasse Vallas)

Above The first prototype MiG-29 first flew in 1977, in the capable hands of the late Alexander Fedotov, who was killed in a flying accident in 1984. This historic aircraft has recently been retired to the Museum of the Air Force at Monino, near Moscow. The prototype has its nose gear located much further forward than production examples of the MiG-29, a 'fault' shared by the prototype Sukhoi Su-27

Left An early production or pre-production MiG-29 in the air. The large ventral fins fitted to early aircraft were found to be unnecessary, and were not fitted to later production aircraft. By contrast, early Su-27s lacked these fins, which were added to production examples of the Sukhoi fighter

АВИАЦИЯ
И
КОСМОНАВТИКА

9

1 9 8 7

With Frontal Aviation

АВИАЦИЯ и КОСМОНАВТИКА

10
1988

ISSN 0373 — 9821

Below Mikhail Waldenburg, Deputy Designer General of the Mikoyan Design Bureau, claimed at Farnborough that the single barrel 30 mm cannon fitted to the MiG-29 is the lightest aircraft gun in the world. Laser ranging apparently makes the gun phenomenally accurate, as the Mikoyan OKB designers discovered during early firing trials. The computer repeatedly shut off the gun after only four or six rounds had been fired, but the targets were still being destroyed. The MiG-29's fold-down ammunition box is located just in front of the nose gear

Above Kitted up in tightly laced, primitive-looking pressure suits, these Frontal Aviation pilots compare notes after a comparatively rare high altitude intercept mission. The sophisticated radar fitted to the MiG-29, and the IRST have a good look-up capability against high flying targets, and the powerful R-33D engines can take the MiG-29 to its ceiling of 56,000 feet in minutes

Below This was the first intercept photograph of a MiG-29 released by the Swedish Air Force. The Soviet pilot was not very co-operative, and refused to 'pose' for the Saab JA-37 Jaktviggen which performed the intercept. The 'Fulcrum' carries a full load of missiles, but those on the inboard stations look too big to be the AA-10 *Alamo* usually associated with the MiG-29. Many analysts believe that the aircraft was actually carrying the AA-9 *Amos*, the Soviet AIM-54 Phoenix copy previously seen only on the MiG-31 *Foxhound*

Right Released a few weeks after the previous photo, this picture, again snapped by a Swedish Viggen pilot, gave the West its first view of a fully armed *Fulcrum*. This aircraft carries a pair of AA-10 *Alamo* semi-active radar homing, BVR missiles inboard, and a single AA-8 *Aphid* on each of the four remaining pylons. The AA-10 bears a close family resemblance to the earlier AA-7 *Apex*, albeit with reconfigured control surfaces. A long range fuel tank is also visible, nestling between the engine nacelles

Left Soviet President Mikhail Gorbachev's policy of *Glasnost*, or openness, resulted in a series of inspection visits by senior US politicians and military men to inspect Soviet weapons systems *in situ*, with reciprocal visits by Soviet personnel. This fully armed MiG-29 was seen on the ramp at Chalovsky AFB, near Moscow, during one such visit

Below left The auxiliary air intake louvres on top of the wing leading edge root extensions are spring loaded to close flush with the skin, but will open to suck in air whenever they are needed, for example during high alpha or knife-edged flight. The front of the AA-10 *Alamo* missile, with its unusual trapezoidal fins, is clearly visible under the wing. Outboard are a pair of *Aphids*

Right Another view of the MiG-29 at Chalovsky. This aircraft was one of the original MiG-29s, with the original narrow chord rudders, although it lacked the ILS aerial under the nose. Another similar aircraft was on view when Defense Secretary Frank Carlucci went to Kubinka to view the Tupolev Tu-160 *Blackjack*

The Red Star of Farnborough

Left 15.00, 30 August 1988: landing lights ablaze, a MiG-29 single seater and a MiG-29UB combat trainer are seen on final approach to Farnborough's Runway 25, about to become the first Soviet fighters to land in Britain. The appearance of the two MiGs at Farnborough was a remarkable exercise in aeronautical *Glasnost* as well as marking a new Soviet desire to market its defence products more widely

Below The MiG-29UB '*Fulcrum*-B' was flown to Farnborough by Roman Taskaev, with Yuri Ermakov in the rear seat acting as navigator for the pair of aircraft. A semi conformal fuel tank is just visible between the engine nacelles. The two MiGs flew from Moscow to Farnborough with a single refuelling stop at Wittstock, a Soviet MiG-29 base in East Germany. Their route took them via Coltishall, Cambridge, and Brize Norton, before continuing west of the busy London TMA to Farnborough itself. Over the Midlands the weather was cloudy, and the Tornados moved into close formation during the descent (*Tony Paxton*)

On arrival at Farnborough, although the skies were grey and overcast, the MiGs led two of the No 5 Sqn Tornadoes in a formation flypast, to the delight of the waiting pressmen. By comparison with the two Tornadoes the MiG-29s left a thick smoke trail, with the single seater smoking more heavily than the UB. Despite their long, and doubtless tiring transit flight, the MiG pilots were determined to arrive in style, perhaps aware that the last Soviet military aircraft to land in Britain was the Tupolev SB.2 used by Molotov to attend a conference in November 1941

Above Three Panavia Tornado F.3s
from No 5(F) Sqn, based at
Coningsby in Lincolnshire,
accompanied by a VC10 tanker from
the Brize Norton-based No 101 Sqn
were on hand to escort the two
Soviet fighters on the final leg of
their journey to Farnborough (*Tony
Paxton*)

Right East meets West: the single
seat MiG-29 *Fulcrum* in formation
with one of the B No 5(F) Sqn
Tornado F.3s. The Tornado crews
complimented MiG-29 pilot Anatoly
Kvotchur on his steady flying as the
formation leader. Rumours that No
5(F) Sqn were chosen for the escort
job because of their red insignia
have yet to be confirmed! (*Tony
Paxton*)

The two MiG-29s were intercepted at Flight Level 420 as they reached the boundary of the UK Flight Information Region, high over the North Sea. Three Tornado fighters were guided onto the MiGs by the Sector Operations Centre at Neatishead, using their own AI.24 Foxhunter radar to complete the intercept (*Tony Paxton*)

Above When the Tornado escorts broke away, the two MiG-29s performed a brief formation aerobatic display, maintaining a rock-steady formation as they flung their aircraft through a series of horizontal and vertical manoeuvres

Right The two MiGs remained in tight formation for the whole approach and landing, with Kvotchur in the single seater trailing slightly behind Taskaev and Ermakov in the trainer. As they passed the control tower, and the famous black sheds, the sun managed to find a gap in the clouds (*R L Ward*)

Below As the two aircraft touched down Kvotchur and Taskaev deployed their braking parachutes simultaneously, with a final touch of slick professionalism

Right The MiG-29UB taxied in first, its canopy cracked open slightly for ventilation. The forward view from the rear seat wasn't bad by Soviet standards, and could clearly be improved by using a retractable periscope. The tiny radome for some type of simple ranging radar was perhaps the most obvious external difference by comparison with the single seater

Left The arrival of the MiGs drew a succession of airborne watchers, including a camera equipped Puma helicopter from nearby RAF Odiham, a Canberra PR.9 of No 1 PRU, and this elderly Vickers Viscount, operated by the Radar Research Squadron of the Royal Aircraft Establishment

Left Like the MiG-29UB the single seater carried a previously unseen version of the Mikoyan OKB (Design Bureau) badge in blue and gold on the low slung engine intakes. The aircraft were not sanitized export machines, but retained *Odd Rods* IFF aerials, an IRST ball, and other operational equipment

Below As soon as they had parked the MiG-29s were surrounded by engineers who had arrived earlier, on the An-124, diplomats and 'minders' from the Soviet Embassy, a pair of British motorcycle cops, and Her Majesty's Customs and Excise who were quick to ask the MiG pilots whether they had anything to declare! One of the Tornado escorts can be seen landing in the background

The three Mikoyan OKB test pilots received a warm welcome from the Press and TV crews, and Kvotchur explained in halting English how pleased they were to be in England. From left to right: Roman Taskaev (pilot: MiG-29UB), Anatoly Kvotchur (pilot: MiG-29), and Yuri Ermakov (pilot/navigator: MiG-29UB). Kvotchur flew most of the demonstrations at the show, alternating with Taskaev, and appeared quite regularly on British television during Farnborough week

Right As soon as they had landed, the Tornado crews were introduced to the Soviet test pilots. Here Wg Cmdr Euan Black, 'Boss' of No 5 Sqn, shakes hands with Kvotchur, while his navigator, Sqn Ldr David Bennett, and the crew of the other aircraft, Sqn Ldr Tony Paxton and Flt Lt Roly Tomlin, look on. With the formalities over the aircrew were soon watching the Mirage 2000 practising its display noisily overhead, and busily comparing notes and swapping stories

Left The Soviet pilots wore an embroidered OKB badge on the left sleeve of their smart dark blue flying suits with the colourful badge of the Communist Party of the Soviet Union on the right breast

Below left The badge of the Mikoyan Gurevich design bureau, as carried on the intakes of both MiG-29s at Farnborough. The badge incorporates a stylized wing with the word MiG in Cyrillic script

Below The visiting aircraft and their escorts were parked in front of the press centre, while the Russian pilots cheerfully submitted themselves to the first of many interviews by the Western media

The angular looking *Fulcrums* made an interesting contrast with the sleek and streamlined Tornado F.3s, as they sat on the taxiway at Farnborough

Left A head-on view of the MiG-29 gives a good impression of the sheer bulk of modern fighters, although the MiG is not considered to be a large aircraft, being about midway between the F-16 and the F/A-18 in size. The huge underslung air intakes, wing leading edge root extensions and centreline drop tank are readily apparent in this view

Above A head-on view of the MiG-29UB disproved early Western speculation that its cockpit might be covered by separate sideways hinged canopies. Although described as a combat trainer, the MiG-29UB lacks the NO-193 pulse Doppler radar fitted to the single seater. The MiG-29UB's small nose-tip radar is probably a simple range-finder

Fighting *Fulcrum:* Showing its Paces

Left Many magazines described the single seater as being a 'MiG-29A'. This designation had absolutely no basis in fact, the Soviet designation not being revealed. One likely designation for the version displayed at Farnborough is simply the MiG-29M (*Modifikatsirovanny*, or modified) or MiG-29*bis*, (Mk 2)

Below The two MiGs spent each night on the north side, parked beside the An-124, and all three aircraft were towed across to the static aircraft park every morning. The MiG-29 is apparently designed to be compatible with all NATO ground handling and support equipment, so that in wartime, the aircraft could operate from a captured airfield without waiting for the arrival of Soviet tractors, starter units, refuelling bowsers and the like (*Chris Allan*)

Left The two Tumansky R.33D turbofans push out pounds of thrust in full afterburner, giving stunning acceleration. Kvotchur and Taskaev were eager to point out that they were not using full power on take-off or during their displays (*Tom Wakeford*)

Below As the MiG-29 accelerates towards rotate speed, shock diamonds are clearly visible in the afterburner flame. Intermediate trailing edge flap and leading slat increase the amount of lift being generated by the wing and dramatically reduce the take-off run

Left The MiG-29 demonstrated an incredibly short take-off run of about 240 metres at Farnborough. This was about half the distance required by the rival F-16. Kvotchur and Taskaev were usually getting airborne as they reached the 'piano key' markings at the end of the runway. The intakes are still firmly closed as the aircraft rotates

Right Great care must be taken rotating the MiG-29 on take-off, since the clearance between the jetpipes and the runway is tiny. The afterburners leave a glowing carpet of flame on the runway as the aircraft takes off

Right Kvotchur 'cleans up' fast after take-off, with the flaps, slats and undercarriage already retracting. The MiG-29's nosewheel retracts rearwards while the mainwheels pivot and swing forwards into the wing root/fuselage fairing

The intake doors can just be seen
swinging upwards into the open
position as the MiG-29 roars into the
air. The huge, widely flared wing
root leading edge extensions give
the MiG-29 a distinctive hooded
appearance, and suggest that the
OKB may have been influenced by
Lee Begin's contemporary Northrop
YF-17

With 'burners blazing Taskaev pulls the MiG-29 into the first manoeuvre of the display, a loop demonstrating minimum height loss on the recovery. The aircraft's incredible agility, despite the lack of a fly-by-wire control system, is due largely to advanced aerodynamics. The Mikoyan test pilots explained that stick forces actually become progressively lighter with increasing G

A high angle of attack flypast is *de rigueur* for the latest fighters at Farnborough nowadays. Kvotchur and Taskaev flew the MiG-29 down to 25 units of alpha, and an airspeed of 190 km/h but emphasized that this left a great safety margin. Like the F/A-18 the aircraft is capable of achieving much higher angles of attack without departing from controlled flight

Left Tight turns with 90 degrees of bank gave onlookers an excellent view of the MiG-29's plan view. For its display the aircraft was fitted with four of its six underwing pylons, although no stores were carried

Below Kvotchur used afterburner and leading edge slat to reduce his turn radius, and was able to keep his display within a very small area. Roll control is by powerful conventional ailerons, which have a wide range of travel

The ailerons can be seen at their
stops as Kvotchur pirouettes his
aircraft in a rapid roll reversal

The second manoeuvre of the MiG-29 display, and perhaps the most
memorable ever seen at Farnborough, was a vertical climbout followed by a
tailslide and whip stall back into the downward vertical. At Farnborough, the
pilots demonstrated a tailslide from 800 metres, but were quick to explain that
this was almost double the normal entry height. This self-imposed safety
restriction was a result of the Ramstein tragedy. The manoeuvre
demonstrated the controllability of the aircraft and the tolerance of its engines

Vapour streams off the wings as Kvotchur racks the MiG-29 into a wickedly tight turn. The engines were remarkably tolerant of hard manoeuvring, running steadily in conditions that would have caused many powerplants to surge or flame out (*Patrick Bunce*)

Below This view of the MiG-29 pulling into the vertical clearly shows how the vortices are generated by the widely flared leading edge root extensions

Left The louvred overwing air intakes are clearly visible, hanging open as Kvotchur turns in towards the crowd line

Above A knife-edged pass was flown down the entire length of the Farnborough runway. During this pass the aircraft accelerated from 450 to 750 km/h, and gained height slightly. The powerful engines and fuselage-generated lift were clearly sufficient to support the aircraft almost indefinitely!

Above Pictured just before touchdown the MiG-29 is seen passing the bright red BAe Hawks of the RAF's Red Arrows aerobatic team. Russia's 'Red Banner' team is apparently equipped with the MiG-29, but we can only hope that they might one day display at a Western airshow!

Above right Taskaev deploys his braking chute just before touching down, killing off his excess speed while not exceeding the landing attitude limitation. This isn't a standard operational technique, but it is a useful way of reducing the landing speed and the landing roll

Right On a couple of occasions the Soviet pilots deployed their brake chutes so early that they were fully open while the aircraft was still many feet above the runway

Above The large cruciform brake chute fitted to the MiG-29 can be seen clearly in this view of the aircraft just before it touches down after another gruelling display

Below Smoke streams away from the mainwheel tyres as the MiG-29 touches down. The energy absorbing low pressure tyres, rugged undercarriage, powerful brakes and large drag chute combine to allow the MiG-29 to be pulled to a stop after a remarkably short landing roll

Overleaf The tiny amount of clearance between the bottom of the jet pipes and the runway surface can clearly be seen in this shot of the *Fulcrum* landing. This must present some problems during operation from uneven, semi-prepared forward airstrips

Uchebno Bitva-Combat Trainer

Right The MiG-29UB is described by the design bureau as a combat trainer, and it carries the IRST system, laser rangefinder and full ECM fit

Below Like the single seat MiG-29 the two seater was towed across to the static park every morning, although it didn't fly a single display during Farnborough week. The fences which extend forward from the tail fins of the single seater are not fitted to the UB. These house upward firing chaff and flare dispensers (*Robbie Shaw*)

The extended canopy fitted to the UB, showing the retractable periscope just behind the central canopy arch. View forwards from the rear seat is poor by Western standards

COCKPIT

The instructor's periscope can be seen in the extended position in this view of the MiG-29UB on finals. Such retractable periscopes are a common feature on two seat training versions of Soviet jet fighters

Left The MiG-29UB taxies out to qualify its display routine during the week before the SBAC show. Both Kvotchur and Taskaev were qualified by the SBAC's Flying Control Committee to fly their routine in either aircraft, although the two seater was apparently not cleared by the Soviets to perform tailslides at display heights (*Denis J Calvert*)

Above Taskaev hauls the MiG-29UB into a tight turn immediately after take-off while practising his bad weather display, which omitted the vertical manoeuvres and concentrated on demonstrating the aircraft's agility in the horizontal plane

Walk-around

Left Before doing his external checks, Kvotchur got into the cockpit to make sure that various switches were made safe. To get out of the cockpit gracefully he used an almost gymnastic manoeuvre

Right The cockpit ladder for the MiG-29 incorporates a brush to remove snow or mud from the pilot's boots! Level with Kvotchur's left boot is the gun barrel and flash suppressor

Left The nose oleo carries a pair of steerable nosewheels. These are fitted with a small mudguard, despite the FOD protection afforded by the intake doors. On production MiG-29s the nosewheel has been moved further aft than its original position on the prototype, almost directly beneath the ejection seat

Above Close examination of this photo reveals the identity of the MiG-29's pulse Doppler intercept radar (NO-193, but spelt here in Cyrillic as 'HO-193'); also the AOA sensor vane on the side of the nose, the Earth connector, the three *Odd Rods* IFF antenna and broad UHF aerial under the nose

The uneven length tripole aerials above and below the nose of the MiG-29 serve the SRZO-2M IFF system, code-named *Odd Rods* by NATO because of the configuration of the antennae. The glass dome in front of the windscreen houses the optics for the infrared search and track system, and for the collimated laser rangefinder. The latter is used against ground and airborne targets. Mikhail Waldenburg claimed that the IRST offered more accurate angular tracking capability than radar, and that the laser gave more accurate ranging information

The underwing weapons pylons fitted to the MiG-29 are extremely crude. The outboard pair, which were fitted to the aircraft seen at Farnborough, are used to carry the AA-8 *Aphid* or AA-11 *Archer* infrared homing air-to-air missiles

Above The wingtips house conventional navigation lights, red to port and green to starboard. Aft of these on each wingtip is a spherical antenna for the radar warning receiver system

Below left Landing lights are mounted on the top of the nosewheel oleo and on the two main landing gear doors. The mounting is crude in the extreme, but effective enough

Right The single pressure refuelling point is located in the port main undercarriage bay. The aircraft can use T-1, TC-1 or PT aviation fuel. The Western designations of these fuel grades are unknown

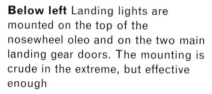

SINGLE-POINT FUELING
UNIT (FUEL T-1, TC-1, PT)

GROU.

FUELING TEST AND
CONTROL PANEL

Above Stencilling on the tail fins gives a good idea of the construction of the MiG-29. Large portions of the fin, including the leading edge and the fairing under the rudder, bear the warning

'Attention, carbon plastic', while other areas are marked 'Care, Honeycomb'. The general surface finish is a little bit agricultural, reflecting the enormous strength built into the aircraft

Right Kvotchur boards his aircraft on Farnborough's north side before taxiing out for a display

The distinctive concentric jet pipes
of the MiG-29 are thought to
contribute to the aircraft's low noise
signature. Cooling air is believed to
pass between the cold stream outer
nozzles and the inner nozzles

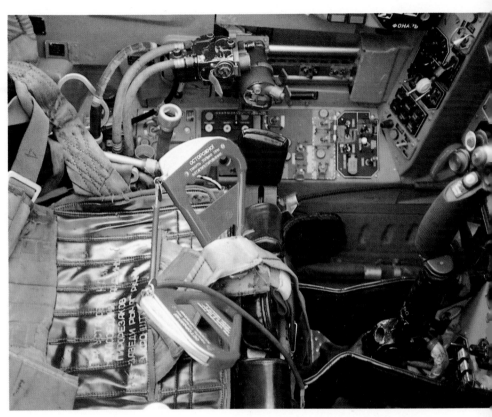

Left An overhead view of the cockpit of an early MiG-29 *Fulcrum*, pictured during a visit by US politicians and USAF officers to Chalovsky airbase near Moscow. The MiG-29 cockpit is fairly standard, having conventional analog instruments and the classic arrangement of control stick and rudder pedals. Not surprisingly, the cockpit has much in common with the earlier MiG-23 *Flogger* and late model MiG-21*bis Fishbed*, a feature which not only simplifies production engineering but also facilitates pilot conversion

Above The ejection seat is actuated by a pair of seat pan handles. The pilot arms the seat by squeezing the triggers, then ejects by pulling the handles. The side-by-side throttles are mounted on piggy back slides on the side of the cockpit and incorporate the airbrake, flap, and other controls

Above The leg restraint system of the MiG-29 consists of a pair of bands which lie flush against the bottom of the instrument panel in normal use, making leg restraint garters unnecessary. The control column is very long, giving the pilot excellent leverage. The stick has at least seven different controls to operate the radios, radar, gun, missiles, chaff/flares and ECM, giving true HOTAS (Hands On Throttle And Stick) capability

Left The MiG-29 has several
uniquely Soviet instruments,
includinc a combined artificial
horizon and turn and slip indicator
(bottom left of this picture). Above
this is the combined AOA and G
meter, which are red lined at 26
degrees AOA and 9G respectively

Above The MiG-29 office is well laid
out and the instruments are easy to
read. The Head Up Display Unit has
a rather narrow field of view by
comparison with the latest Western
HUDs, but it is highly regarded by
Soviet pilots, who praise the simple
and easily understandable way in
which it presents complex data

Farewell
Fulcrum

Below This pair of BAe Sea Harrier FRS.1s taxied out just before the two MiGs, accompanied by a third Sea Harrier. Following their departure, the Sea Harriers made a wide orbit of the airfield, timing their return over the far end of the runway to coincide with the departure of the two MiGs

Right The MiG-29s wound up to full dry power before releasing their brakes. Kvotchur, in the single seater, following Taskaev and Ermakov in the UB. For the long transit flight home both aircraft had their underwing pylons removed, and long range fuel tanks were mounted between the engine nacelles

Left The aircraft took off with full dry power, which gave a slower rate of acceleration and a rather longer take-off run. The intakes, as always, were closed off by the massive intake doors until well after the nosewheels had lifted. In dry power each aircraft left a thick smoke trail (*R L Ward*)

Main picture The departure of the two MiG-29s on 12 September 1988 left many people wondering what the Soviets would send to Paris in 1989, and to the next Farnborough. Most agreed that the MiG-29s would be a very hard act to follow (*R L Ward*)

Left The weather was not kind to photographers hoping to record the departure of the MiGs, with thick low cloud and very little light. The two Sea Harriers slid into position on the wings of the MiGs straight after take-off, with the third Sea Harrier standing off to take photographs of the unique formation. The Soviet delegation had expressed great admiration and respect for the Sea Harrier, and the MiG test pilots and the pilots of No 899 NAS had struck up an unlikely friendship. This was celebrated by a low level, high speed beat up of Farnborough before the MiGs finally turned for home

Overleaf The MiG pilots eased their aircraft lower and lower for their final flypast, and although there were only three or four photographers present, our shutters were clicking as furiously as they had done during the week!

103

Foreign *Fulcrums*

Indian test pilots became the first foreigners to fly the aircraft when they evaluated the MiG-29 in 1985, and that year India became the first export customer when it signed a contract for the delivery of 48 MiG-29s for delivery in the April and May of 1987. The first Indian MiG-29 unit to form was No 47 Sqn, 'The Archers', based at Poona

Like fighter pilots everywhere the Indians take great pride in being able to fly a good, steady, close formation. It's not very tactical, but it looks pretty on a photograph, especially against snow covered mountain scenery!

Overleaf The Himalayas provide a dramatic backdrop for this MiG-29 of No 28 Sqn. The Indian Air Force is the fourth largest in the world, and is rapidly becoming one of the best equipped. The pilots of No 28 Squadron are confident that in the MiG-29 they have an aircraft capable of tackling any likely adversary with ease. The MiG-29 is known as the Baaz (Falcon) to the Indian Air Force

Left The Indian Air Force owes its
organizational structure, rank
system, traditions and even its
uniforms to its original close links
with the British Royal Air Force.
Here, groundcrew prepare a MiG-29
of No 28 Sqn, Indian Air Force, for a

training sortie. No 28 Sqn, otherwise known as 'The First Supersonics' are proud of their history as India's first MiG Squadron, having become the first unit to receive the MiG-21 in April 1963

Main picture In the air defence role Yugoslav MiG-29s will carry the K-13A, B and M family of IR homing air-to-air missiles known to NATO as *Atoll* as well as the more modern R-60/AA-8 *Aphid* dogfight missile. Some sources suggest that the new AA-11 *Archer*, designed as a replacement for the AA-2 and AA-8, is already in Yugoslav service

Above The MiG-29's short take-off and rough field capabilities make it the ideal fighter for the Yugoslav Air Force, which frequently practises off base operations from a host of minor airfields around the country. Underground shelters at the major air defence bases were built for the MiG-21, and are consequently too small for the newer aircraft

Right Delivery of the MiG-29 to Yugoslavia represents the most important element in its programme to upgrade its air defence organization, the *Ratno Vazduhoplovsto i Protiv-Vazdusna Obrana*, or RV-PVO. Ordered in 1986, the first MiG-29 Regiment supplements three air defence regiments equipped with the MiG-21bis and MiG-21*bis*-K

Left Yugoslavia has watched with anxiety as neighbouring countries, particularly Greece, have upgraded their air arms. Introduction of the MiG-29 has given the Yugoslav Air Force a fighter aircraft in the same class as the newly delivered F-16s and Mirage 2000s of neighbouring Greece

Below left In Yugoslav service the MiG-29 is known as the L-18, with the letter L standing for *Lovac*, or Hunter. The serial number on this aircraft shows it to be the first of the original batch of eighteen aircraft supplied to Yugoslavia from October 1987

Below Although Yugoslavia is working on an advanced fighter of indigenous design, the *Novi Avion*, the Yugoslav Air Force is set to take delivery of two further batches, 16 each of MiG-29s, during the next two years. If the indigenous aircraft does not go ahead, the MiG-29 seems certain to be ordered in even larger numbers to replace the ageing fleet of MiG-21s

Below Yugoslav MiG-29s will have an important secondary ground attack role, using indigenously produced UV-12-57, UV-16-57 and UV-32-57 rocket pods, and S-240 unguided missiles. Other air-to-ground weapons in the Yugoslav inventory include the AGM-65 Maverick and AS-7 'Kerry' air-to-surface missiles The pilot of this Yugoslav MiG-29 wears a squadron badge on the front of his Soviet-made flying helmet. Yugoslavia's MiG-29s made their operational debut at the large international air show and exhibition at Batajnica during the summer of 1988

The first batch of 16 MiG-29s
delivered to Yugoslavia has been
used to form a new fighter regiment,
and not to re-equip an existing
MiG-21 unit. The MiG-29s will be
used in conjunction with
Yugoslavia's new AN/TPS-43 air
defence radar to strengthen the
country's air defence network

Encore!

Red Star Rising: the MiG-29, gears travelling, accelerates in full afterburner before its famous tailslide manoeuvre (*Patrick Bunce*)

In the MiG-29, Mikoyan have produced yet another world class fighter. It is doubtful whether the MiG-29's stupendous agility can be improved upon unless the bureau's next product features full-authority fly-by-wire. Check six!

This page and previous three pages With full afterburner selected Anatoly Kvotchur pulls the MiG-29 into a tight turn directly after take-off on the final day of Farnborough '88. Although weather conditions were perfect he decided to fly his flat, 'bad weather' display, demonstrating for the first time the MiG's amazing manoeuvrability in the horizontal plane. Kvotchur flew with verve and enthusiasm, giving the huge crowds probably the most impressive display of the entire show

Last page Roman Taskaev piles on the G as he flicks his MiG-29 into a wickedly tight turn, indicated by the healthy puffs of vapour (*Chris Allan*)